The Global Marketplace

Business Without Borders

Globalization

David Andrews

Heinemann Library
Chicago, Illinois

www.heinemannraintree.com
Visit our website to find out
more information about
Heinemann-Raintree books.

To order:

☎ Phone 888-454-2279

🖳 Visit www.heinemannraintree.com
to browse our catalog and order online.

© 2011 Heinemann Library
an imprint of Capstone Global Library, LLC
Chicago, Illinois

Edited by Adam Miller and Andrew Farrow
Designed by Ryan Frieson
Original illustrations © Capstone Global Library
   Ltd 2011
Illustrated by Planman Technologies (India) Pvt
   Ltd
Maps by Mapping Specialists, Ltd
Picture research by Hannah Taylor

Originated by Capstone Global Library Ltd
Printed and bound in China by South China
   Printing Company Ltd

15 14 13 12 11 10
9 8 7 6 5 4 3 2 1

**Library of Congress Cataloging-in-Publication
Data**
Andrews, David.
  Business without borders : globalization / David
Andrews.—1st ed.
     p. cm.—(The global marketplace)
  Includes bibliographical references and index.
  ISBN 978-1-4329-3933-5 (hc)
  1. International trade. 2. Globalization—Developed
countries. 3. Globalization—Developing countries.
I. Title.
  HF1379.A728 2011
  658'.049—dc22   2010004097

Acknowledgments

The author and publisher are grateful to the
following for permission to reproduce copyright
material: Alamy Images pp. **29** (© Photogenix),
31 (© imac), **43** (© Bill Bachmann); Corbis pp.
4 (dpa/Friso Gentsch), **8** (Louise Psihoyos), **17**
(Gideon Mendel), **34** (James Leynse), **37** (Reuters/
Jagadeesh), **39** (Jim Richardson); Getty Images
pp. **19** (AFP/Bay Ismoyo), **20** (Darryl Leniuk),
33 (AFP Photo/Carl De Souza); Photolibrary
pp. **6** (The Print Collector), **13** (Geri Lavrov), **15**
(Tetra Images), **25** (Marili Forastieri), **41** (Caroline
Penn), **45** (age fotostock/Jose Enrique Molina);
Rex Features pp. **11** (Richard Jones), **27** (Sinopix/
Richard Jones), **49** (Jason Alden).

Cover photograph of the PSA Singapore Terminal,
the world's largest container port, reproduced with
permission of Getty Images (Stone/Eightfish).

We would like to thank Michael Miller and
Laura J. Hensley for their invaluable help in the
preparation of this book.

Contents

Some words are printed in bold, **like this**. You can find out what they mean by looking in the glossary.

The World at Your Fingertips

The world used to seem like a much different place. A century ago most people could only learn what was happening around the world from books and newspapers. People were just beginning to travel across the world on trains and boats, but the journey could take weeks. The clothes people bought and the food people ate were usually made nearby, or even at home. A **consumer** (buyer) in New York City could barely imagine what might be happening in China, let alone watch its news on television, put on a shirt that was made there, or think of a product to sell there. Distant places seemed very far away.

It's a small world

Today, the world is right at your fingertips. You can "visit" those faraway places without leaving your living room. You can follow news around the world on your television. You can talk to people across the world on a cell phone. You can share a funny story, pass around photos of your family, or debate an important point with anyone in the world with a click of a mouse. Products from around the world are available, too. Just about anything you could want is for sale through the Internet.

Globalization

These changes in the way the world interacts are known as **globalization**. *Globalization* refers to the way technology has connected people and businesses around the world into a single marketplace.

The German carmaker VW recently started a plant in India, where costs are cheaper.

It no longer matters as much as it once did what country you are in or how far businesses are from their customers or employees. Thanks to technologies such as the Internet, air travel, and satellites, products and **services** from around the world are available. These products and services are made by companies operating and trading in many different countries, employing workers of many different nationalities. This trade spans the globe (see chart below).

MAJOR EXPORTERS OF GLOBAL PRODUCTS	
Product	**Country**
Rice	Thailand
Oil	Saudi Arabia
Diamonds	South Africa
Computer software	United States
Cars	India
Cocoa beans (for chocolate)	Ivory Coast
Textiles	China

Benefits of globalization

At first glance, these new connections sound like a good thing. And in many ways they are. They give businesses more customers. When businesses compete with each other, they may need to drop their prices to win customers. These low prices benefit the consumer, as does having more products to choose from. Workers may enjoy more flexibility, as technology allows them to avoid moving to where the jobs are—and people may even be able to work from home.

The drawbacks of globalization

However, globalization has drawbacks as well. For businesses, too much competition can cause them to lose customers or to shut down altogether. For consumers, too much competition might mean that your favorite local store will go out of business because it cannot compete with a huge international brand. For workers, as their companies struggle to compete, they might find themselves laid off and replaced by workers in countries where workers are paid less. Finally, if we are not careful, the environment may suffer as **pollution** gets worse as a result of more businesses forming and growing (see pages 44 and 45).

Globalization and you

Globalization does not necessarily make life better or worse, but it does make it more complicated. This book will try to untangle the complex web created by our increasingly connected world. By understanding the benefits and drawbacks created by globalization, you can become a better-informed consumer in the **global** marketplace.

Becoming Global

Globalization did not happen overnight. It is the result of a process that has been happening for centuries. In the early stages of human history, people lived in small groups. Each group mainly did everything for itself. People grew their own food, made their own clothing, and built their own homes. The goods that each group created varied depending on where they lived. For example, people near oceans did more fishing, while people in warmer areas grew fruits. Some groups created new kinds of clothes, tools, or other inventions that their neighbors had not thought of.

Discovering trade

Over time, some groups began to trade with their neighbors. It began with nearby people, but eventually they began to trade with people from faraway places. They found that some groups had better soil for growing different crops, and that others had become skilled at creating certain products, such as dishes or tools.

Trade benefited everyone involved. Thanks to trade, each group had access to more products and could learn from what others were doing. It was no longer necessary to do everything oneself. Instead, people could spend time creating the products that they were particularly good at, while trading for the other goods they needed.

By the early 1800s, ports like this one in Bordeaux, France, were bustling business centers.

Powerful trading nations

As technology improved, the trading opportunities grew. Ships sailed all over the world, and the countries that traded the most often grew the wealthiest. Private companies began to trade all over the world.

Some of this trade benefited everyone, but other trade took advantage of poorer nations while benefiting richer nations. For example, some European nations began trading their goods for African people, whom they forced into slavery. They used these slaves to develop lands in their new territories in North and South America. This further increased European wealth compared to poorer nations.

Globalization takes off

Fast-forward to the 20th century. Over the decades, telephones, airplanes, and computers made it even easier for companies to sell their products across borders. Companies, mainly in the United States and Europe, began opening offices, stores, and factories in other countries.

For these **multinational** companies, it became less important what country they were based in. They realized that they could move different parts of their operations to different parts of the world. Many factories moved to countries where labor was cheaper.

Some companies even moved their headquarters to other countries, often because the **taxes** were lower there. Without a single country to call home, they became truly global **corporations**.

What is globalization?

Globalization can mean many things. To many **economists**, it refers to the increased flow of **goods**, money, people, and work across the world, thanks to improved technology and fewer barriers. In a completely globalized world, the following processes can occur:

- Goods can be easily traded between one country and another, and people all over the world have access to goods from all over the world.
- People can move freely from one country to another to live, work, or visit.
- Money, or **capital**, is invested around the world, not just in the country where the money was earned.
- Modern technology is available throughout the world, and communication technology allows information to flow freely.

Are all of these things happening today? Not everywhere. There are still many barriers to **immigration**, for example, and much of the world does not have access to modern technology. Globalization is not a goal that we have reached, but a process that is still ongoing today.

Doing what they do best

People around the world disagree about whether globalization is a force for good or harm. Supporters often point to **economic theory**. This refers to the ideas that explain how economies work. Economic theory suggests that increased trade improves life for all its participants.

Comparative advantage and opportunity cost

Many economists say that globalization benefits the world by encouraging each country, and each person, to do what they do best. The idea is that different countries and communities are better suited to certain activities than others. They can do these things better, less expensively, and more efficiently than they can do other things. This is known as **comparative advantage**.

One way to think about comparative advantage is to consider what activities a country or community must give up when it decides to produce something. What you must give up is called **opportunity cost**. For example, say you have one hour after school. You could shovel the snow off the sidewalk of your neighbor, for which she will pay you $10, or you can use the time to play video games. What is the cost of each activity? The opportunity cost of one hour of video games is the $10 you could have earned, and the opportunity cost of shoveling snow is the one hour of fun you would have had playing games.

Countries also pay an opportunity cost when they choose to do one thing instead of another. But how do countries decide what to produce? They do so by using their time to produce the product with the lowest opportunity cost, doing what they do the best, and then trading with another country to get what they do not produce.

Different countries are better suited to different kinds of work, like this factory work, due to factors such as costs and **resources**.

A beneficial trade

A simple example can show the benefits of comparative advantage and trade. Imagine two people, Ellen in Canada and Marcos in Spain. They can use their time to make two things: bicycles and chairs. Now, let's pretend that Ellen and Marcos have exactly the same resources they can use to build the chairs or bikes: one day, one factory, and one pile of raw materials for each of them. Because of the differences in their countries, it takes each a different amount of time or resources to make each product:

USING THE SAME RESOURCES...			
Ellen can make	20 bicycles	or	5 chairs
Marcos can make	10 bicycles	or	1 chair

In this case, the opportunity cost to Ellen of producing 20 bikes is the 5 chairs she will not be able to produce, and the opportunity cost to Marcos of producing 1 chair is the 10 bikes he will not be able to produce.

Absolute versus comparative advantage

Thanks to technology in her country, Ellen can make more chairs and bikes than Marcos. This means that she has an **absolute advantage** in both. Absolute advantage means you are able to produce more output with the same inputs as someone else. But, does this mean that Ellen should make both bikes and chairs, and that Marcos should make nothing? The surprising answer is no, and this is where comparative advantage comes in. When you look at the numbers you see that Ellen is twice as good at producing bikes as Marcos, but she is five times better at producing chairs as Marcos. Since we know that you should do what you are best at, we can conclude that Ellen should spend her time producing chairs, and let Marcos spend his time producing bikes. Then each can trade for the product they do not have.

WHAT THEY PRODUCE	
Ellen	**Marcos**
Ellen produces 5 chairs at an opportunity cost of 20 bicycles.	Marcos produces 30 bicycles at an opportunity cost of 3 chairs.
She trades them to Marcos for 30 bicycles. She is 10 bicycles ahead.	He trades them to Ellen for 5 chairs, coming out 2 chairs ahead.

The realities of trade

According to many economists, everyone should benefit from globalization, because it gives people and countries the opportunities to do whatever gives them a comparative advantage. However, the realities of the world paint a more complicated picture, as we will see throughout this book.

Displaced workers

When a country focuses on doing what it can do most efficiently (giving it a comparative advantage), some people lose out. That is because the country eliminates those **industries** that do not give it a comparative advantage. As a result, people who worked in these industries might lose their jobs to someone in another country. (See pages 32–35.)

An uneven playing field

Both businesses and countries can tilt global trade to their advantage. Some corporations can grow as powerful as the countries in which they operate. Companies that are spread out over many countries can be difficult to **regulate** (see box below). Countries can also create an uneven playing field. And many countries push for an end to trade restrictions that do not benefit them, while keeping in place those restrictions that do (see page 41).

Why regulate?

Throughout history, governments have passed laws that regulate business, meaning they control how it operates. These **regulations** have been necessary to protect a variety of groups.

Some regulations protect workers. Before western countries had **labor unions**, workers were often treated unfairly and did not benefit at all from a company's success. By uniting together to form unions and threatening to slow down production or strike (stop working altogether), the workers had a stronger voice. They could then often get higher wages and benefits like health insurance. Many western governments passed regulations requiring companies to allow workers to organize in this way and protect their rights.

Regulations can also protect other businesses. Regulations and regulatory groups have been needed to keep big businesses from overpowering smaller companies and forming a **monopoly**, meaning a huge company that is so powerful it prevents competition.

Other regulations and regulatory groups have been created to ensure that the products being manufactured and sold are safe (see pages 28 and 29) and that claims in advertising are accurate. These regulations protect the consumer.

In more recent history, governments have begun to pass regulations to protect the environment. Laws prevent businesses from causing too much pollution or cutting down too many trees, for example (see pages 44 and 45).

Rising inequality

The result of globalization's uneven playing field is that some countries, and some people, benefit more than others. For example, people who live in cities are better able to get to globalized jobs than people in rural areas. People with technology such as Internet connections can connect to the rest of the world, whereas people without technology cannot.

In addition, the benefits to the world's wealthiest people often seem much greater than the benefits to the rest of the world. The incomes of the world's wealthiest people are growing faster than the rest of the world. They see the greatest benefit of economic growth.

Many western clothing companies have moved their factories to China, where young women like these work long hours for little pay. This saves the companies money, but some critics worry that the trade-off for these savings is unfair conditions for the workers.

Trading Around the World

Global trade is all about buying and selling. One person sells and another person buys. One country **exports,** or sells goods to another country, and another country **imports**, or buys goods from another country.

But what is bought and sold, and at what price? It is all related to **supply** and **demand**.

Supply and demand

The laws of supply and demand are the key to **economics**, or the study of how people use money and resources. Supply tells you how many goods someone is willing and able to sell at the going price. Demand tells you how many goods people are willing and able to buy at the going price. But what happens when the quantity supplied and the quantity demanded are not the same? The price changes.

Say the going price of a coat is $100. At that price, a U.S. **producer** (person who makes a product) is willing and able to sell 100 coats (the quantity supplied), because he will make a good **profit**. The problem is that the quantity demanded is only 50 coats, so the supplier has 50 coats left over. To help clear out his rack full of coats, he may lower his price to $75. At the new price, the quantity demanded may rise, allowing him to sell the rest of his coats. The price at which the quantity demanded and the quantity supplied are equal is known as the **equilibrium price.**

Enter global trade

Globalization has a big effect on supply and demand. For example, if a company in China can afford to make and export coats to the United States much more cheaply than the U.S. company can make them, the Chinese company can afford to sell them at a lower price. This causes prices to fall. If the U.S. company wants to keep selling coats and compete with the Chinese company, it will have to lower prices or find a new way to make coats more cheaply.

The Chinese coat company might have been making coats for Chinese people before at a low price. But if it finds it can export coats for a higher price, it might not be willing to sell them for the same low price it used to sell them for in China. If the company raises its prices in China, the Chinese might choose not to buy the company's coats. The demand there will drop.

What is the result of all these developments? The Chinese company ends up with U.S. money. The U.S. consumer ends up with cheaper coats. The U.S. business loses customers, and the Chinese consumer may lose out on inexpensive coats.

Container ships like this carry enormous amounts of goods across the world, helping supply the products of global trade.

Trade imbalances

In an ideal world, every country would find an equal number of things to buy and sell to each other. But we do not live in an ideal world. Often one country will be able to sell a large number of goods to another country, but will not want to buy a lot of goods from that country. This is known as a **trade imbalance**.

Why trade imbalances happen

Trade imbalances can happen for many reasons. One reason is that a certain country can produce goods more cheaply, often due to lower wages paid to workers (see page 11).

Another factor is the value of **currency**. The values of different currencies change in relation to each other all the time. If at a certain moment the U.S. dollar is worth more in the global marketplace than the Chinese yuan, then Chinese businesses will be willing to sell their goods for fewer U.S. dollars. This translates to cheaper prices for U.S. consumers, so they will buy a lot of Chinese goods. In this same situation, U.S. businesses will need to charge more Chinese yuan for their goods, and as a result they will sell fewer goods because the price is too high.

Trade deficits and surpluses

As a result of these factors, some countries end up importing more goods than they export. This means they have a **trade deficit**. Other countries export more than they import, resulting in a **trade surplus**.

Economists disagree on whether trade deficits are a problem. The potential problem seems obvious—when you have a deficit, your money is going to another country, and you are not producing as much as you use. A trade deficit seems to make a country poorer and put it in a weaker position in the world marketplace.

Investment

However, trade deficits have their benefits. For example, a portion of the U.S. trade deficit with China is due to the fact that China is profiting from investing in the United States. China buys financial products such as U.S. Treasury bonds, which provide money for U.S. businesses and government. That money can be used to build new businesses, roads, or complete other major projects in the United States. But eventually, the United States will have to pay back the money that was invested.

A variety of products

Second, a trade deficit means that consumers in the importing country are buying more products. (That is why the products are being imported!) Those products are not being bought in the exporting country, often because their wages are too low.

WHAT IT MEANS TO ME

Strong and weak currencies

What is the benefit of a strong currency? You can see it most clearly when you visit another country. Say you go to Japan and bring $1,000 with you. Based on an exchange rate of 100 yen to the dollar, you can convert it into 100,000 yen. Because the dollar is strong, you can stay at decent hotels and buy lots of goods to bring home.

But what if you go back a year later, and the dollar has weakened compared to the yen? You can only exchange your dollars for 80,000 yen, or 80 yen per dollar. Your dollar will not go as far, so you will not be able to buy as many goods or stay in the nicer hotels. You will lose out, and so will the Japanese businesses that will not be getting as much money from you. Meanwhile, back home in the United States, Japanese tourists will be able to buy more with their yen, benefiting businesses there.

Corrections

Finally, some economists argue that trade deficits correct themselves. Remember the example on page 13 of the currencies of the United States and China? When the U.S. dollar is more valuable than the yuan, then Chinese companies are willing to export goods to the United States for a lower price in U.S. dollars. In the same way, consumers from China can buy more with their currency.

But if the trade deficit continues, more and more of that Chinese currency will pile up in other countries, making it less valuable over time. Exporters will demand more currency for their goods, and Chinese consumers will be able to buy less with their currency. Eventually, some people argue, the trade deficit will balance out.

What's the value of a dollar?

So, how much is money worth, anyway? The best way to measure the value of a currency is to look at what it buys. Purchasing power is the measure of how many goods can be bought with a given currency. To determine purchasing power, economists select a constant (stable) group of goods, such as clothing, medical care, and transportation, and calculate how much they would cost in each country.

Knowing purchasing power helps determine the wealth of a person or a country. To determine how wealthy people are compared to people in another country, for example, you cannot just look at how much money they earn. You have to look at what they can buy with the money they earn, which is their purchasing power.

Exchange rates show how different currencies compare to each other, as seen on this display. But they don't tell the whole story of how much money is worth.

Breaking Down Barriers

It used to cost a lot more to trade internationally, both in terms of time and money. A century or more ago, people needed a good reason to buy something from a faraway country. This was because they would have to pay much more to have it shipped back home and would have to wait a long time for the ship to come in. For most things, it made more sense for people to buy something made nearby, or even to make it themselves.

In recent times, shipping goods by air or by sea has become cheaper, faster, and easier. Passing information around the world has become virtually free, too, thanks to the Internet. But there are still some costs to trade—some inevitable, and others set up by people.

Trade barriers

As we have seen, if other countries are exporting goods to your country, the people who make those same kinds of goods in your country may lose their jobs. So, to protect their own workers, governments often try to make it cheaper and easier to buy products made at home. They can do this with **trade barriers** such as **tariffs**, **subsidies**, and **quotas**.

Tariffs

A tariff is a fee that importers must pay for every good they import. Tariffs raise the cost of goods that are imported. This helps local businesses compete with low prices from foreign businesses.

Subsidies

A subsidy is money that governments give to local producers of goods. As these subsidies give the producers extra money to live off of, they can therefore afford to charge a lower price for the products they sell. These low prices give them an advantage over foreign competition.

Quotas

A quota is a limit on the number of a type of good that can be imported to a country. Quotas ensure that a certain number of goods will have to be made at home to meet the demand of consumers.

Effects on trade

While these trade barriers may help workers at home, they can have negative effects on people in other countries. Since these actions give an advantage to products made locally, they make it harder for other countries to export goods to that nation.

These measures can also affect consumers at home. Tariffs and quotas might raise the price of a good locally, since cheaper foreign goods are prevented from being sold in the country. Local producers do not have to compete with low prices from overseas.

Subsidies can make it possible for producers to sell their goods more cheaply than their competition. Since a government is paying for some of the cost of production, the producers can afford to sell goods at a lower price and still make a profit. They can export their goods around the world for low prices, and local producers in other countries may suffer.

Haiti's rice problem

One example of the problems of tariffs and subsidies can be found in the Caribbean island nation of Haiti. There rice farmers have found it impossible to compete with cheap imported rice. Tariffs and subsidies have been blamed for the problem.

In the 1980s, most of the rice eaten in this poor nation was grown at home. But in the interest of promoting **free trade**, Haiti lowered its tariffs on imported goods. The tariff on rice was lowered to 3 percent—lower than the rice tariffs in other Caribbean nations. That made it cheaper for rice to be imported to Haiti. To make matters worse, rice growers in the United States were receiving government subsidies, making it even cheaper for them to produce rice. Haitian farmers, who did not receive any subsidies, found it impossible to compete.

In Haiti, one of the poorest nations in the world, people have few alternatives to growing rice. Some farmers began to grow other crops. Others were forced to abandon their fields. Many moved to cities in Haiti or to other countries nearby in search of work.

Rice farmers in Haiti, like these men, struggle to make a living due to their government's efforts toward free trade.

17

Reducing protective measures

We think of the modern era as a time of free trade, meaning that there are fewer costs to trading than ever before. However, there are still many barriers to trade. Most countries use measures such as tariffs, subsidies, and quotas to protect some of their industries.

Leaders of many countries agree that they would be better off trading in a world without such protective measures. The problem is that if they were to remove these measures on their own, their local industries would suffer. This is because goods could be imported more cheaply to their country, but if other countries did not adopt similar policies, local producers would not be able to successfully export more goods to other countries.

For that reason, countries protect themselves by making agreements to all reduce measures such as tariffs, making it cheaper to import and export goods.

The GATT

After World War II (1939–45), many countries were looking to encourage more trade, in order to help their economies rebuild from the war. They agreed to reduce tariffs, quotas, and other restrictions on global trade. The General Agreement on Trade and Tariffs, or the GATT, was signed in 1947 by 23 countries.

As years passed, more countries joined the list, and more changes were made to make trade freer. By 1994 more than 120 nations had signed on to the GATT, and the countries agreed that a formal organization should be formed to deal with world trade issues.

The World Trade Organization

In 1994 the nations that had signed on to the GATT formed a new international organization called the World Trade Organization (WTO). Like the GATT, the WTO works to reduce restrictions on free trade such as tariffs and quotas. The organization also requires its members to use the WTO to resolve trade disputes, rather than negotiating with countries on their own. But the WTO has many critics (see box at right).

Treaties between nations

Smaller groups of nations called **trading blocs** have also worked to increase trade through treaties.

CARICOM

The Caribbean Community, or CARICOM, was formed in 1973 to economically integrate 15 Caribbean nations and resolve trade disputes among them.

EU

The formation of the European Union (EU), in 1993, reduced trade restrictions on member nations and made trade even easier by introducing a single currency (the Euro) that most member nations use.

NAFTA

The North American Free Trade Agreement (NAFTA), formed in 1994, allows freer trade between the United States, Mexico, and Canada.

Criticism of the WTO

While organizations such as the WTO were created to promote trade between countries, many people argue that they have favored richer nations over poorer nations. Protestors have demonstrated outside WTO meetings, arguing that the agreements made at WTO meetings favor wealthy nations and corporations. They say that poor workers such as farmers and factory workers in poorer nations, like the Haitian rice farmers on page 17, are being **exploited**. They say that more measures need to be taken to protect the poor workers most affected by globalization. (For more on these criticisms—and the WTO's reactions—see pages 46 and 47.)

In 2009 these protestors organized in front of the Trade Ministry in Jakarta, Indonesia, to protest the effects that global trade—and WTO agreements—have had on poor workers throughout the world.

Globalization and Business

Imagine you are the owner of a skateboard company entering this new era of globalization. For years, your business has been profitably selling skateboards by providing good quality at a fair price. You have a factory where your employees work hard and are paid well for their work. You have a supplier who sells you wood from trees made in another part of your country. You make a comfortable, but not enormous, profit each year.

If everything were to stay the same, you might want to just keep your business as it is and continue making your comfortable profit. But if there is one thing successful business owners know, it is this: if you are not moving forward, you are moving backward. This is even more true in an era of globalization.

People who run businesses, like this skateboard company, must make a lot of difficult decisions if they want to compete in the global marketplace.

Keeping up with the competition

What happens if you stick with "business as usual"? Thanks to globalization, you now have more competition. A skateboard company across the ocean could begin selling skateboard decks in your country. Because they have a factory in China where wages and prices are lower, they can afford to pay their workers less. They also buy their wood at a discount from a South American company, so it costs them about 25 percent less to make each skateboard. Their boards are not as good, but many people look only at the price and switch to your competitor. Even worse, many skateboard companies have begun advertising their products online. People can order products from all over the world. If there is another company out there that makes a product as good as yours for a better price, or better than yours for the same price, then you are likely to lose sales. Unless you are the world's best, most efficient skateboard maker, you will never be safe.

How do you compete?

In this new world, you must compete or risk going out of business. Fortunately, globalization offers you the same opportunities that it offers your competition. You can start by launching a website to sell your product around the world. This will introduce your product to new markets and give you the opportunity for more profits.

However, you discover that the competition's prices are lower than yours. To cut costs, you reduce the comfortable salaries you pay at your factory. As a result, you soon find your workers quitting and being replaced by less experienced, less reliable workers. In the end, you have to close your factory and move it to a country where you can hire workers more cheaply.

You try think of other parts of your business you can do more cheaply. Perhaps you can buy your wood from a cheaper international supplier. Or maybe you can hire someone in another country to run your advertising or customer service for a cheaper price. In the end, you find yourself auctioning off your work to the lowest bidder. And with a world of people looking for work, the bids can be very low.

Costs and benefits

In this example, there are costs and benefits all around. Globalization has cost people in your local community who have seen well-paying jobs disappear. But it has benefited those places where the jobs have moved— and those areas may need the work even more.

The new markets you have tapped into online will also benefit from having the option of buying your skateboard. Your existing customers may benefit from having a less expensive product available. However, if you have been forced to compromise on quality in order to reduce prices, then they may end up losing out as well.

Corporations seeking new markets abroad

Capitalism is an economic system in which private individuals and corporations—rather than governments—produce and control the means of production, such as farming and factories. In a capitalist system, what most businesses want more than anything else is to grow. For some big corporations, globalization is the best path to growth.

These companies have grown so large that they have expanded as much as they can at home. They may already have a store or an office in nearly every area of their home country. They may have already beaten the competition at home, but that is not enough.

Wal-Mart

The biggest retail store in the world is Wal-Mart. By the 1990s this U.S. company had stores in every area of the United States. So, in order to grow and improve its profits, Wal-Mart looked abroad.

Answering to shareholders

The need for growth is partly affected by shareholders. A shareholder is someone who has bought a share, or a **stock**, of a company. All shareholders are part-owners of the business, and they make important decisions about the operation of the business. The main goal of shareholders is to see the value of their stocks rise. If the profits of the company go up, the price of the shares will rise, and the shareholders will make a profit. The only way for company profits to go up year after year is for the company to grow.

Wal-Mart needed different strategies for different countries. The stores proved unprofitable in some countries, such as Germany and South Korea, so the company closed locations there. In Japan and India, the company teamed up with local companies. It did this in order to get around regulations that limit the amount that a foreign country can invest. The company opened an office in Moscow, Russia, to break into the Russian market, while in Chile it purchased a series of local retail stores.

Wal-Mart now has more than 3,400 stores internationally, making up more than one-quarter of its **revenue** (the money made after goods are sold), according to *The Wall Street Journal*.

HSBC

The UK bank HSBC, one of the world's largest companies, has its own strategy for global growth. Rather than focus on expanding further in wealthy, or **developed**, nations (see page 26) such as the United States, Australia, Japan, and European nations, HSBC focused on "emerging markets."

These markets are in countries that are not fully developed with modern technology and industry, but that are rapidly growing due to the effects of globalization. (See the map below for the locations of these developed and emerging markets.)

One reason for this strategy is that businesses are not growing as rapidly in countries such as the United States, where banking options are everywhere. But countries in South America, Asia, and the Middle East are growing more rapidly as they benefit from increased global trade. In 2004, 60 percent of HSBC's revenues came from the seven most-developed nations in the world. By 2007 the majority of its revenues came from less developed, but faster-growing economies.

As this map shows, many parts of the world are "emerging markets" that companies like HSBC can continue to explore for business.

"The World's Local Bank"

Even with its operations in developed nations, HSBC is trying to take advantage of globalization. The bank focuses on working with businesses and other clients that have strong connections internationally, particularly in emerging markets. By focusing on its connections all over the world, HSBC hopes to create efficient ways for global businesses to do banking.

HSBC has learned one lesson of globalization. Although the world may be more connected than ever, each market and country is different. While one business model might work for the United Kingdom, a different one is needed for Egypt or Thailand. That is why the bank has focused on knowing the local markets and culture of each area it expands into. Its goal is to be "The World's Local Bank."

Advantages for small businesses

Big businesses are not the only ones to benefit from globalization. New connections between the world's markets have also opened doors for small businesses. The rise of the Internet has made it possible for these small businesses to reach customers across the world without spending much money. With a good distribution and payment system in place, all a small business needs to do is create a web page. Then anyone with an Internet connection can learn about the business and buy goods and services from it.

WHAT IT MEANS TO ME

How to start an international business

Could you be a global businessperson? Starting an international business can be challenging, but with today's technology, almost anything is possible.

Creating a product

The biggest challenge is finding a unique product that you can sell around the world. Let's say you are a great cartoonist. You draw a picture of a dog wearing a funny hat that everyone seems to love. Perhaps other people will love it, too. You decide to sell products that feature your unique drawing.

First, you need to create a product. You might search online for a T-shirt company that can make lots of T-shirts with your design on them for a low price. Make sure they can make it in different colors and sizes!

Getting it online

The next thing you need is a website. It helps to have a web address that customers will remember. For example, if www.funnydogwithahat.com is available, you might try to register that address, meaning to make it officially yours. Next, you will need to design your website, creating pages that allow customers to search for the T-shirt they want. They will also need a way to pay for it. Using an online payment service like Paypal makes it easier to do this.

Once your website is online, it will be possible for people around the world to check out your T-shirts. More people will discover your site if you advertise online. But if you want to sell your products to them, you will also need to know the tax laws in each country where you sell a T-shirt. You can start with your own country and then expand to other countries as your business grows!

And larger companies have found that small businesses and even individuals can compete with them in a global market. For example, Greer and Associates, a major company that makes commercials and takes photographs for catalogs, learned this firsthand. In Thomas Friedman's book *The World Is Flat* (2005), Greer and Associates owners Jill and Ken Greer explained how individuals are able to compete with them. These individuals can reach customers all over the world through the Internet. They can also use the latest computer technology to create products that look just as professional as what a larger company can produce. Many customers find that **freelancers** do just as good work as large companies can do, but at a cheaper price.

People who start their own businesses and work from home can be increasingly competitive in the global marketplace.

Pluses and minuses

Being a small business can have its advantages in a changing world. Most small businesses don't have the money to make big investments around the world or to advertise heavily. However, a small business may be able to adapt quickly to changes in technology or consumer demands. Having fewer decision-makers makes it easier to make big decisions. In a rapidly changing world, that can be a big advantage.

Globalization and the Developed World

For the nation's wealthiest countries, also known as the developed world, globalization can have its benefits and its drawbacks. As we have seen, each country can focus on what it does best and most efficiently, and offer those services to countries around the world. The effects of globalization are also felt on a smaller scale by consumers and businesses.

What is the developed world?

There is no universal definition for the *developed world*. Sometimes economists refer to some countries as being "more economically developed countries" (MEDCs). These countries enjoy high incomes **per capita** (per person) and have a high **Gross Domestic Product** (GDP) per capita. GDP is a measure of the total value of products and services produced in a country in a year.

HIGH-INCOME COUNTRIES	
Luxembourg	Denmark
Norway	Canada
Singapore	Australia
United States	Germany
Ireland	United Kingdom
Switzerland	Finland
Netherlands	Belgium
Austria	Japan
Sweden	France
Qatar	Equatorial Guinea

There are many ways to examine countries. One is by looking at the income per capita of a country's population. This is computed by dividing a country's GDP by its population. This chart shows 20 countries with a high income per capita.

These countries, which include the United States, Canada, Japan, Australia, United Kingdom, and many European countries, have more advanced technology and industry than the rest of the world. They also typically have higher levels of education than other countries—although some less economically developed countries, such as India, also have a highly educated workforce (see page 37). A country can also have great resources and wealth, but not be developed because the wealth is not used to improve society. In many nations with great oil wealth, for example, a small group of leaders grows very wealthy, but the money is not used to build schools and roads or to provide economic opportunities for the population.

Benefits for consumers: More variety

For the consumer in the developed world, the benefits of globalization are obvious when you go shopping. Walk down the aisle of the grocery store and you will see evidence of the benefits of global trade. Many of the products available are produced in less economically developed countries. For example, bananas are grown in tropical climates and imported to the United States, Canada, Europe, and other areas. So is most coffee, which is made in countries like Brazil, Colombia, and Indonesia. Without global trade, these products and others simply would not be available. And countries such as Japan, which has limited land for farming but a large population, depend heavily on food grown in other countries.

One effect of globalization is an incredible number of choices for the consumer, as seen in this electronics store in Japan.

Lower prices

Globalization also lowers the price of many products. It does this for two reasons. First, more businesses are able to compete for business in a globalized world. The business that wins customers is often the one that offers the lowest price.

Second, businesses are able to lower their costs by producing their products in less expensive ways. For example, take a company that produces socks in France. In the past, it might have hired French workers to produce socks in its local factory. But those workers might have been paid $30 USD (U.S. dollars) per hour. These workers may also be paid other benefits and be difficult to fire because of strong labor unions. Regulations in France might also add to the cost of producing socks. All of these expenses go into the cost of producing each sock, and the costs are added into the price of the socks.

Buying online

You experience the benefits of the global marketplace anytime you shop online. Type in a product you want into a search engine, and you are likely to find dozens of options available to you. Some may be local, while others may be from around the world.

Imagine life before the Internet. You would have always shopped at your local stores, and you often would have had little choice except to pay what they were charging. Now you can choose from products from around the world being offered online, choosing the one that fits your exact need at the best price.

However, if the business moves its factory overseas, the cost of producing the socks becomes less. If the socks are manufactured in a less economically developed country, workers can be paid less and offered fewer benefits. Being less developed may also mean that there are fewer regulations within the country. The lower costs and fewer regulations make it cheaper to produce each sock, and therefore make it possible to offer the product at a lower price.

Drawbacks for consumers

While globalization certainly offers benefits to consumers, it also causes its share of problems.

Problems with quality and safety

As discussed earlier (see page 10), regulations are sometimes put in place to make businesses behave in a safe, fair way. In many developed countries, there are regulations that create strict safety standards for products made there. Groups such as the U.S. Consumer Product Safety Commission enforce these regulations by charging fines and creating penalties when companies break the rules. While problems do sometimes happen, these regulations and enforcing groups lead consumers to feel secure that they will buy safe products.

But many large corporations choose to move their factories and other operations to **developing** nations (see page 36), where costs are much cheaper. Often these developing nations have far fewer regulations in place. This lack of regulation can sometimes lead to products that are harmful to consumers. While in theory these products should be caught before being sold in the developed world, dangerous products often slip through and cause harm.

Spread of diseases

The flow of products from one country to another has another unintended consequence. Those products may be carrying harmful substances such as diseases and pests. When they are exported to another country, these unwanted arrivals can spread.

For example, when bovine spongiform encephalopathy, or mad cow disease, began to spread in cows in the United Kingdom in the 1980s, it spread to other countries when they imported British beef. This disease has led to the deaths of more than 160 people in the United Kingdom over a 15-year period. As a result of the disease, the United Kingdom had to destroy large quantities of beef, and other countries were forced to closely monitor their beef supply and destroy some imported beef.

The spread of "mad cow disease" from British beef made people aware of a negative side of globalization.

Benefits for businesses

For businesses in the developed world, globalization provides opportunities.

More customers

First, thanks to globalization, businesses have far more places in which to sell their products and market their services. For those businesses that take advantage of new markets and customers, the result is higher profits. Many companies that have expanded as much as they can at home have found that expanding into new countries is the only way to keep growing. And, as we have seen, the goal of most businesses is to grow.

Lower costs

Running a business in a developed country can be expensive. Land is more expensive, taxes can be high, and the cost of employing workers, including salary and related benefits, can eat away at total profit. If companies can find ways of moving part or all of their operations to other countries where these costs are less, they can improve their profits and pass these savings on to consumers as lower prices. Moving parts of a business to another country is sometimes known as **offshoring**.

Some businesses have done so much offshoring that it is not clear exactly what country is "onshore." In other words, they do not seem to have a single country to call home anymore. In some cases, a company might even move its headquarters to another country where taxes are lower.

Diverse talent pool

Companies that are not based in a single location are no longer forced to hire workers who live nearby. For many kinds of work, they can draw on talent from all over the world. They can hire **consultants** who can improve their operations, employees who can do work from home without the expense of an office (see page 32), and freelancers around the world who can take on projects inexpensively.

Many businesses have turned to businesses in other countries for **outsourcing**, or hiring another company to do work for it. This allows companies to focus on the parts of the business that they do best and leave other parts of the business to others.

Drawbacks for businesses

The pitfalls of globalization for businesses in the developed world can be summed up in one word: competition. Competing businesses from around the world can cut into a company's profits, forcing it to find new ways to cut costs in order to keep up.

Outsourcing the drive-through

Some fast-food companies have found an unusual way to make globalization work for them. Rather than having employees in their restaurants take the orders of customers who use the drive-through, they outsource it. When a customer places an order, the message is not sent into the store, but rather to another part of the country or even across the world, where a worker talks with the customer over a phone line and types in the order on a computer. The order is then sent to the workers in the store, who prepare the food.

This experiment has been tried in U.S. stores such as McDonald's and Jack in the Box. The goal is to allow employees in the store to focus on food preparation and ringing up orders, which business owners hope will speed up the operation and leave customers more satisfied.

Competitor benefits

From the point of view of a business, the benefits of globalization have one big problem: everyone benefits from them. This makes competing businesses that much harder to compete against.

For example, if Company A is taking advantage of offshoring to cut costs, then it can cut its prices and take away customers from Company B. As a result, Company B has to cut costs just to keep up. And if Company A is taking advantage of the Internet to attract talent from around the world, it may find ways to make a better product than Company B can produce.

The end result is that for businesses in the globalized world, there is little margin for error. Work must be done efficiently and effectively in order to survive, and the company that finds the way to create the best product for the lowest price is often the one that wins out.

Benefits for workers

Do workers in the developed world benefit or suffer from globalization? It depends on what industry people are in, and how able they are to adapt to the changing times.

One of the greatest benefits of the interconnected world is the ability to do work for people anywhere in the world, from anywhere in the world. If people work in an industry in which their work can be delivered online or over phone lines, then today's technology makes it possible to work from almost anywhere. Mobile devices allow people to check email while traveling. Computer technology allows them to send files and even hold video conferences with people around the world.

Workers can also compete for jobs not only at home, but also around the world. Then again, people from around the world can compete for jobs in someone else's hometown!

Homesourcing

The practice known as **homesourcing**, or employing people who work from home, is growing more popular. In the United States, more than 20 percent of workers spend at least some of their time at home. Having employees who work from home cuts down on costs such as office space and utility costs for the business and its clients.

One example of a company that uses homesourcing is JetBlue Airways. If you call the airline to make a reservation, the agent you speak to is working from home. Rather than outsourcing the job to workers overseas, the company employs people like stay-at-home mothers who work from home. Employees appreciate the flexible work opportunity, and the company says the system is efficient and effective.

Drawbacks for workers

But the move to globalization also poses many risks for workers. Globalization has caused many people to lose their jobs, as jobs are shipped overseas to places where the same work can be done less expensively.

Factory workers

Some of the hardest-hit workers are those who work in factories. Many businesses have found it more profitable to move their production facilities overseas, where both land and labor are less expensive.

The people left behind find themselves out of a job. As more and more factories move overseas, these people have nowhere to turn. In a globalized world, it often does not pay to keep factories in developed nations. Former factory workers are forced to start over in a new industry and learn new skills to compete in the modern job market.

Worker protests

When jobs have been lost due to offshoring, workers and communities have often protested. For example, in the United Kingdom, workers protested when clothing manufacturer Burberry closed a local plant. And thousands protested in Belgium when plans were made to close a factory manufacturing Opel cars.

In France, protests have turned violent. In 2009 car-parts manufacturer New Fabris went **bankrupt**, meaning it was unable to pay its debts, forcing the layoff of hundreds of workers. Some workers, angry about the compensation plan (the money given after they were laid off), threatened to blow up the factory.

In the end, the workers negotiated a new compensation plan, but the threat was copied when other French factories closed. Other French workers who were laid off have turned to "bossnapping." They held their bosses hostage until their company agreed to offer a better compensation plan.

In 2007 these protestors gathered outside Burberry's London store. They were protesting the company's decision to close down a British factory and ship the jobs overseas.

The auto industry

One of the industries hardest hit by offshoring has been the auto industry. Detroit, Michigan—formerly the home of the U.S. auto industry—has seen its unemployment rate soar and its population shrink as factory after factory has left the area for Mexico and other countries. Unemployment passed 17 percent in 2009, more than any major U.S. city, and economists said the only way for unemployment to drop

Car factories in Detroit like this one have become empty as a result of the recent economic crisis.

was for more people to move away. The city known as "The Motor City" no longer had enough jobs to support its population.

U.S. automaker General Motors (GM), facing big losses due to global competition and a **recession** (decline in economic activity), planned in 2009 to close as many as 20 factories in Michigan, Indiana, Ohio, and Delaware. GM-owned car companies in Europe also faced troubled times. Vauxhall, based in the United Kingdom, and Opel, based in Germany, were targeted for possible cutbacks as well.

Toyota plants

While many automakers have been relocating factories to less developed countries in recent years, Japanese company Toyota has opened factories both in the United States and United Kingdom. In the United States, Toyota has opened factories everywhere from Fremont, California, to Georgetown, Kentucky. In the United Kingdom, Toyota manufactures more than 270,000 cars each year.

Developed countries offer strong **incentives**, such as tax breaks, to attract companies such as Toyota to set up operations locally. Having a factory boosts the local economy, creating well-paid workers who will spend money in other areas.

Toyota benefits as well. By having a local plant, the company can avoid the fees required when goods are imported from Japan. Also, the United Kingdom had set a quota, or limit, on the number of cars that Toyota could import. By building some of the cars in Derbyshire, England, Toyota found an effective way to sell more cars in the country.

Threats of relocation

Even if a factory does not close, the threat of offshoring can reduce the benefits workers receive. Corporate leaders often negotiate compensation with labor unions. Corporate leaders can offer workers a choice: accept fewer benefits, such as payment, health care, and **pensions** (retirement payments), or the factory may be moved overseas. In many cases, employees are willing to accept less if it means saving their jobs.

For example, German car company Daimler recently planned to relocate some of its manufacturing to the United States, angering many German workers. When they protested, Daimler decided to slowly reduce its workforce by offering early retirement and part-time work to many of its employees.

WHAT IT MEANS TO ME

Careers in a globalized world

How does globalization affect your future career? Some industries are disappearing thanks to globalization and may never return, while others are likely never to disappear. It all depends on whether your job can be outsourced or offshored.

If you do manual labor that someone in another country could learn to do, or if your job does not require a lot of education, your job may move overseas. Even some high-skilled jobs are outsourced today. For example, many information technology jobs are outsourced to India because workers in the country have high levels of education.

On the other hand, jobs that require the worker to be in a specific place, such as a chef or a firefighter, will never be outsourced. And you are also more likely to keep your job if you have a skill that will be hard to learn in a developing country. In the future, it will be more important to have a high level of education and to specialize in something. That will make you harder to replace. But as industries continue to change, you will also need to change, too, by continuing to learn new skills throughout your career.

Globalization and the Developing World

The developing world is made up of countries that have lower GDP per capita and a less developed **infrastructure**. In these places, globalization has provided opportunities as well as problems.

Benefits for developing nations

Many developing nations are able to trade their goods with other countries, and the arrival of multinational corporations has meant more jobs for people who badly need them.

Attracting business

Developing countries go to great lengths to attract business. Many offer financial incentives such as tax breaks. Looser regulations and inexpensive labor further attract businesses. Working conditions are often poor, hours are long, and the pay is a low—often less than $1 an hour. These conditions would never be accepted in the developed world. But for people living in developed countries, these jobs are often the best option available.

For example, at a factory making clothing in Honduras, workers earned $13.10 for a 10-hour day in 2005. Labor rights groups said that the workers were being exploited. But more than 44 percent of workers in Honduras live on just $2 a day— less than one-sixth of what was offered at the clothing plant.

Rising incomes

For many developing nations, globalization has offered a way out of poverty. In 1970, 17.4 percent of the world was living on $1 a day. Today, only 5.5 percent of the world earns so little in today's dollars.

Poor people in China and India have especially benefited. The number of people living in poverty in rural China dropped from 250 million to just 34 million in 20 years. And India cut its poverty rate by one-third in 25 years.

Gaining skills

Workers at factories in developing countries benefit in other ways as well. They gain not only income, but also valuable experience. They learn how goods are produced and pick up important skills. Some companies also hire local workers as managers, so they gain management experience. These skills can help develop a professional culture in a country and make it easier for people to start new businesses locally.

Globalization in India

Many people in India have benefited from globalization. One reason for this is that many of its workers, while earning less money than those in more developed nations, are well educated. This is due to an extensive higher education system. As a result, India has become a center for outsourcing many jobs that require some education.

India has become well known for its call centers. These are businesses in which Indian workers take or make calls on behalf of companies in more developed countries. If you have ever called customer service about a problem with a product or answered a phone survey, you may have spoken with someone from India.

Indian workers are employed in many other globalized jobs as well, from making auto parts to medical transcription (taking audio recordings from doctors and health care workers and turning them into written reports).

These well-paying jobs have boosted incomes among Indians. In fact, as incomes rise, places like India's call centers are finding it more difficult to find qualified workers willing to work for low salaries. They may soon find themselves forced to move to other countries with inexpensive, eager workers.

At a call center in India like this one, workers answer customer service calls for companies from around the world.

Drawbacks for developing nations

Supporters of globalization point out that the jobs it brings to developing countries are better than those that would otherwise be available. But in many cases, the influence of global corporations causes more harm than good.

Child labor

In the developing world, weak regulations often lead to exploitation. Many factories making products for more developed nations have been found to be forcing children to work for pennies a day. For example, in 2006 the National Labor Committee, an organization that fights abuses against workers, found that children had been forced to make clothing at a Gap factory in Jordan. These 10- to 13-year-old children were forced to work 16 hours a day for no wages. If they resisted, they were beaten with rubber hoses. Other multinational companies, such as Wal-Mart and toymaker Mattel, were also found to have children working in their factories.

This is usually done without the knowledge of the parent companies. Often companies send in overseers to inspect the factories just once or twice a year. Local managers know in advance when the inspections will be and can prevent inspectors from learning the truth.

Coffee growers in crisis

For coffee growers around the world, globalization has not provided new skills. What it has done is reduce the already-low pay growers receive by forcing them to compete with the world's least-paid coffee growers.

The problem is that there are many coffee growers around the world, so the people who buy the beans can simply go to the farmer who sells them at the lowest price. In the past, the amount of coffee exported was limited by international agreements, which helped to keep prices up. But the United States pulled out of the agreement, and over time the price of coffee decreased.

As a result, for every pound of coffee, which can cost somewhere between $3 and $9, farmers in 2001 only made 35 cents, and coffee pickers made less than 14 cents. The rest of the money went to the many "middle men" who buy and sell the coffee before it lands on supermarket shelves.

Brain drains

One threat to economic development in many poor nations is the "brain drain." Thanks to globalization, it is easier than ever for people to move from one country to another. As a result, some of the most talented people in a developing nation may leave in search of greater opportunities elsewhere. Too few talented workers are left behind to help improve their society and economy.

Chickens in Chile

Sometimes the line between opportunity and exploitation is hard to see. Take the story of a taxi driver in Chile who quit because he could not earn enough money. He took a job that pays less than $200 a month at a plant that processes chickens for sale in Latin America, Europe, and Asia.

According to a report in the *New York Times Magazine*: "His job is to stand in a freezing room and crack open chickens as they come down an assembly line at a rate of 41 chickens per minute." The cold causes him to lose feeling in his hands, and some other workers are no longer able to raise their arms. But the pay is better than the taxi job, and other workers would gladly take his job if he left.

Working conditions in chicken-processing factories like this one can be grueling—and even dangerous—for employees.

Winners and losers

Every country in the developing world experiences globalization differently. In some countries, many people have seen their incomes increase due to new trade and new opportunities. These countries may benefit from globalization thanks to educated workers, good roads, or a stable political system. Other countries have seen global corporations exploit their resources, but have benefited little from it.

Within countries, too, there are winners and losers. One good example is India. While well-educated workers take calls from around the world in call centers (see page 37), others are not so lucky. Cities are still filled with slums, and many people in villages around India are poor. In fact, more than 300 million Indians live on less than $1 a day. Even in a country that has been called a globalization "winner," many people are losing out.

"Race to the bottom"

In areas where people have benefited for a time from globalization, they can suddenly find themselves on the losing end. This is because, like all businesses, multinational corporations are always seeking ways to increase profits. If they can find a cheaper way to get work done, they will. This has been called a "race to the bottom" as companies race to find the cheapest places to produce their goods.

For example, in Mexico, for decades thousands of manufacturing jobs arrived from the United States, where labor was more expensive. Workers in Mexico earned about $2 an hour. But in recent years, many of those jobs have moved once again, to China, where workers earn just 60 cents an hour.

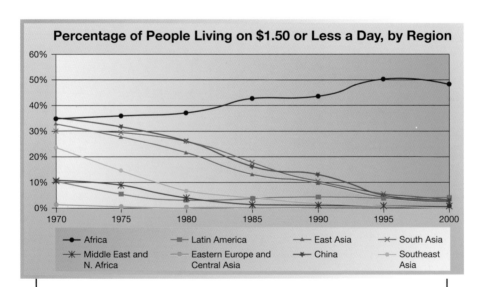

As this graph shows, in many parts of the world many people live on less than $1.50 a day. This has increasingly been the case in China in recent years.

In sub-Saharan nations like Ethiopia, many people have not benefited from the wealth and new technologies that global trade has brought to other parts of the world.

Africans left behind

Though not everyone benefits equally, most countries do see rising incomes thanks to globalization. But the big exception has been sub-Saharan Africa, which has been growing poorer while the rest of the world climbs out of poverty.

Many areas of Africa suffer from low levels of education, political instability and corruption, and major health problems such as AIDS and other illnesses. As a result, many multinational companies have been reluctant to invest in African nations. Multinational companies take resources, such as oil, minerals, and metals, but the country ends up with little to show for it.

For example, Nigeria is a nation rich in oil. Multinational oil companies are in Nigeria extracting oil, which is shipped to nations around the world. The Nigerian government collects most of the money—in fact, more than 80 percent of its revenues come from oil. However, because of corruption, crime, and other problems in the Nigerian government, much of the population has not benefited from this money. Life expectancy and average income in Nigeria have actually declined since 1970.

Anger at globalization

Globalization's effect on the developing world has left many people angry. They complain that owners of big corporations in rich countries benefit most. They argue that powerful businesses use money to influence governments to remove regulations that do not benefit the corporations.

People around the world feel they have little chance to speak against these powerful interests. Many believe that organizations meant to help, like the WTO, actually favor the interests of richer nations (see pages 46 and 47). Leaders of developing nations say that new rules are needed to make sure that everyone can benefit from the promise of globalization.

Making Globalization Work

Globalization today has its believers and its critics. But nobody believes the system works perfectly. People are working to address the many problems associated with global trade, including effects on culture, the environment, and the people most affected by the system.

Cultural effects

Globalization does not just affect economies. It has also had an impact on all aspects of the world, including ideas and culture. When multinational corporations sell the same goods all over the world, and people can buy goods from around the world online, the differences between countries and cultures begins to blur.

"McDonaldization"

Thanks to the successful expansion of major multinational businesses, people across the world have access to some of the same products. Microsoft computer software, Levi's jeans, Apple iPods, and McDonald's Big Macs are available in more and more countries around the world. Critics complain that big corporations (mostly from the United States) are forcing the rest of the world to adopt a common culture, leading to what they call the "McDonaldization" of society.

But how much is the presence of products from more developed nations really affecting local culture? In many cases, companies benefit from adapting their products or business to the local culture. For example, McDonald's is not the same from one culture to another. In Cairo, Egypt, patrons can buy "McFalafel" sandwiches, while McDonald's in India offers burgers made of lamb, because eating beef is against the Hindu religion.

Importing western culture also has its benefits. In East Asia, many people cited the clean bathrooms as one of the best things about McDonald's. Some say this influence has raised sanitary standards in the area.

The globalized media

The spread of information through television and the Internet can also have an impact on the developing world. Today, people in villages from Mongolia to Honduras are exposed to some of the same television programs and movies, many from the United States. Some critics say these images promote western values such as consumption (buying things), rather than traditional values such as family and religion. Also, seeing the vast differences between their own lives and the glamorous lives of people on television can create dissatisfaction and resentment among those who are struggling to survive in a developing country.

This woman in a remote area of Nepal, in Asia, is able to connect to the world through the Internet. Some would say this shows a positive side of globalization.

The spread of information

But the availability of information can also have a good influence on society. Being able to communicate with people around the world can benefit people who were once isolated. For example, in 2009 Iranians protesting the results of a presidential election were able to communicate via social-networking services such as Twitter. Protestors could share their experiences and observations with other protestors, allowing them to coordinate their actions. They could also share their experiences with the rest of the world, drawing attention to their cause.

The spread of information can shine a spotlight on challenges faced by people, such as civil rights issues, government corruption, and hunger. When information about life in the developing world is communicated around the world, people and organizations are driven to help.

Global terrorism

The global spread of culture and information has its dark side. This became clear with the rise of the global terrorist network al-Qaeda. This network of Islamic extremists rose for many reasons, including a belief that U.S. influence was harmful to society. Al-Qaeda feeds off resentment of western culture and the idea that countries such as the United States and United Kingdom are trying to dominate the world, both economically and militarily.

Al-Qaeda also takes advantage of new technology to spread its message and plan attacks. Websites promoting extremist ideas can be accessed all over the world. The ease of air travel makes it easier to create a global network—and to attack other countries. And al-Qaeda leader Osama bin Laden was able to spread his message simply by releasing recordings, which were replayed by television stations around the world.

Environmental effects

The connections between countries allowed by globalization also has consequences for the environment. As the world's economies grow and people continue to consume resources, dangers to the environment have also grown. At the same time, global connections have offered new possibilities for solving these problems cooperatively.

Challenges of growth

One of the great challenges to the world's environment has been the simple fact of human growth and consumption. Capitalism depends on economic growth, which leads people to use more resources and affects the environment in other ways. Globalization has the potential to accelerate this trend, as increased trade leads to faster economic growth.

Developed countries release more carbon dioxide into the air because of the increased output of their factories and their increased need to ship goods. Scientists believe this is causing Earth's temperature to rise. For example, the United States releases nearly five times as much carbon dioxide per person as the world average, and Europe releases about twice as much per person. Less developed areas such as Africa and South America release much less carbon dioxide—but their levels could grow if they develop due to globalization.

Globalization can also accelerate the use of natural resources such as oil and gas. These fuels are used in industry as well as transportation, two key aspects of global trade.

Business practices

Another challenge to the environment is the actions of multinational corporations. Competition can drive businesses to do whatever brings the highest profit, regardless of environmental cost. Globalization increases the number of ways that businesses can get around environmental regulations. If a country's regulations are too strict, the business can simply move to another country. The result is that facilities are often located in countries with loose regulations. This results in higher profits for the business but environmental harm for the host country.

Information and cooperation

There are reasons to hope that the era of globalization will not lead to environmental destruction. The first is the flow of information. Thanks to better technology, it is now much easier to identify and prosecute the companies that are causing pollution. And thanks to the Internet, it is more difficult for businesses to cause environmental harm in secret. Environmental groups can alert the world to destructive practices, leading to **boycotts** and protests if businesses do not respond.

In addition, international agreements can be made to regulate the environment. For example, world leaders have recently embarked on efforts to reduce pollution that contributes to climate change. However, some countries pollute more than others, and more developed nations are more able to reduce pollution than less developed nations. As a result, reaching agreement on such complex issues has not been easy.

Cattle and the Amazon

One of the world's most valuable resources is the Amazon rain forest, located mainly in Brazil. This rain forest is home to thousands of species found nowhere else on Earth. By absorbing carbon dioxide, the rain forest also plays a key role in preventing global warming.

But the growth of industry in Brazil has threatened the rain forest. Thanks to globalization, the country's cattle industry has been able to greatly increase its exports. Multinational corporations buy beef and leather from Brazil to sell around the world. But to continue to grow, the industry cut down trees at the edge of the rain forest. Between 1991 and 2000, more than 170,000 square kilometers (65,000 square miles) of rain forest were destroyed, mostly to make room for more cattle.

However, as more attention has been brought to the destruction of the Amazon, the pace of **deforestation** has slowed. The Brazilian government has protected more areas. Environmental groups have also helped. A 2009 report by Greenpeace exposed illegal deforestation by the Brazilian cattle industry. Consumers have also pressured businesses to react. As a result, companies such as Nike and Wal-Mart agreed not to buy leather and beef from businesses engaged in these practices.

As this photograph shows, parts of the Amazon rain forest have been completely wiped away to make way for industry.

Free trade versus fair trade

In the years since globalization picked up steam in the 1980s and 1990s, a great debate has taken place: Is globalization a force for economic growth and development, and ultimately a good force that will improve lives of people around the world? Or is it merely a tool that the world's wealthiest people and corporations can use to gain ever-higher profits—at the expense of people at the bottom of the economic ladder?

Protesting globalization

Protestors around the world have fought to make sure free trade is fair to all involved. They have many targets. As we have seen, one is the global corporations that profit from free trade—protestors say at the expense of workers and ordinary people around the world.

Another target is the global financial system. This includes organizations such as the WTO (see page 18), the International Monetary Fund (IMF), and the World Bank. Each of these groups was formed to promote economic development, but the way they have done so has drawn criticism, as seen in the chart at right. All of these groups pursue policies that benefit wealthier countries and businesses, and not necessarily developing nations and their citizens, protestors say.

The IMF and the Asian financial crisis

The IMF has been criticized for the conditions it sets on countries that accept its loans (see chart at right). It often requires countries to balance their budgets by raising taxes and cutting spending. While these measures can help put countries on the road to economic health, they can cause problems during times of economic crisis.

In the 1990s, for example, Asia was struck by a financial crisis. Asian nations went into deep recession, currencies lost value, and nations were deep in debt. The IMF lent money to the countries, but required them to reduce their debt and avoid too much spending. However, during hard economic times, government spending is often needed to keep the economy going. With the government unable to help, the recession spread to more countries. Later, during the 2008 financial crisis, governments accepting loans faced similar restrictions that some believed made their financial situations worse.

GOALS AND CRITICISMS OF GLOBAL FINANCIAL ORGANIZATIONS

Organization	Goal	Criticism
World Trade Organization	Created as a forum for countries to negotiate trade agreements. Representatives from various countries work together to reduce trade barriers such as tariffs to promote trade.	Critics say past agreements have been tilted in favor of wealthy countries, allowing them to keep tariffs in place while poorer countries remove trade barriers.
World Bank	Provides loans to developing nations at a favorable **interest rate**, with the goal of promoting development and reducing poverty.	A few powerful countries run the organization. Critics say its development strategies do not work for many countries. Some development projects have also caused environmental harm.
International Monetary Fund	Stabilizes the world economic system by allowing countries to borrow money temporarily when needed. Countries that have too much debt can borrow from IMF to keep their currency stable.	Nations taking IMF funds may be required to cut subsidies, raise taxes, and reduce government debt, which can cause hardship. The IMF has also been criticized for lending to countries run by military dictators.

Responding to criticism

As criticism of world financial organizations has grown, some people are trying to make the global economic system more fair. Following protests in Seattle, Washington, in 1999, the WTO has worked to give more of a voice to developing nations. Recent talks have focused on helping poor farmers around the world by reducing trade barriers that hurt their business. And the World Bank has shifted its focus from economic development projects to reducing poverty around the world.

Finding Solutions

As the world has become more aware of the drawbacks and dangers of globalization, people have come together to find solutions. Some have worked to see that the trade system rewards everyone fairly. Others have tried to make sure that global growth does not mean environmental harm.

Economic summits

As criticisms have been raised about organizations such as the WTO, World Bank, and IMF, world leaders have tried to make the financial system work better. At first, a small group of the world's seven or eight most powerful countries, known as the G-7 or the G-8, met to discuss the financial system. Then it became clear that more countries needed to be included. The G-20, which includes 19 countries plus the European Union, has met to discuss ways to make the global marketplace work better for everyone. In 2008, for example, the group met to discuss the financial crisis occurring in the world that year (see box at the top of page 49). They agreed on ways to help economies grow again and strengthen their financial markets so that similar crises did not occur in the future.

Environmental reform

World leaders have also met in the hopes of stopping economic growth from harming the environment. As we have seen, most scientists believe that people have been harming the environment by releasing carbon dioxide into the atmosphere, which causes the world's average temperature to rise. As a result, ice will melt and sea levels will rise, changing weather patterns and affecting nations around the world.

To prevent this crisis, leaders have met to discuss ways to reduce the amount of carbon dioxide that is released into the air. The results have been mixed, but the fact that people around the world are working together is a step in the right direction.

Fighting unfair practices

Thanks to today's technology, information flows more quickly than ever. This makes it easier for consumers to learn about unfair trade practices in faraway countries. If workers are being treated like slaves or being paid next to nothing, news organizations can spread the word. Informed consumers can respond by not buying from companies that benefit from these practices. And with the help of the Internet, advocacy groups can organize protests and boycotts that push companies to change their practices.

Global recessions

One of the problems of globalization is that the good times are not the only things that become global. Economic problems become global, too. Thanks to the global financial system, recessions that start in one country can easily expand to other countries. For example, the global financial crisis that began in 2007 started mainly in the United States, but spread around the world. In the United States, banks had been lending money (called mortgages) to people to buy expensive homes. Those loans were then sold to banks and people around the world. When people in the United States began to have difficulty paying back their mortgages, people around the world lost money. A problem that began in the United States spread all over the world. Many economies fell into recession. The connections in the global marketplace caused nations to struggle together, just as they rise together in good times.

WHAT IT MEANS TO ME

Buy fair trade

One way you can help make global trade fair is to look for products marked with a fair trade label. This label means that the product has been made by following certain rules. Workers must be paid above a certain amount for their work. Organizations look at what workers are paid before allowing products to be marked with a fair trade label. Consumers who buy a product labeled "fair trade certified" know that the workers have been treated fairly. But because of the higher wages paid, fair trade products usually cost a little more.

In 2009 protesters supporting fair trade organized events like this one in London's Trafalgar Square. They wanted to highlight the importance of buying fair trade bananas.

Looking forward

Globalization is a process that has been going on for centuries, since societies first began trading. Improvements in technology, such as the Internet, satellites, and transportation, have caused the world to globalize more rapidly than ever. In the future, this trend is certain to continue. Goods, money, and information will flow ever more quickly across national borders, making the differences between countries less important. Cultures will continue to mix, resulting in a single world market.

At the same time, however, people will take with them lessons they have learned about globalization. While many people still agree that globalization has the potential to improve economies around the world and reduce poverty, it must be monitored and regulated. International organizations, as well as individuals working together, will be key to ensuring that people around the world experience the benefits of economic growth.

Winners and losers

No matter how fair a system is, there are likely to be winners and losers. Consumers may benefit from a greater selection of goods at lower prices. But the movement of jobs and capital will have consequences for the people left behind. Workers will need to be more adaptable than ever. Governments will need to provide resources to keep its workforce well-trained for the jobs of the future.

Developing nations are likely to encounter new opportunities. The work may often be punishing, with long hours and low pay. But if the promise of globalization holds, living standards will rise over time and better jobs will one day become available. As incomes rise, they will demand more goods from around the world.

In the end, globalization will not solve the world's problems. But if economic development lifts more people out of poverty and helps the world reach its economic potential, the world as a whole will benefit.

Timeline

1945	The General Agreement on Trade and Tariffs (GATT) is formed to negotiate trade rules. The World Bank and International Monetary Fund are also formed.
	World War II ends, making trade between more nations possible again.
1947	The Cold War begins, limiting trade between **communist** and capitalist countries.
1975	Advances in computers, satellites, and electronics make global trade more common.
1988	The Free Trade Agreement, signed between the United States and Canada, takes effect, removing trade barriers between the two countries.
1989	The Berlin Wall falls, leaving capitalism as the world's dominant economic system.
1991	The World Wide Web is created, allowing greater global communication.
1992	The North American Free Trade Agreement (NAFTA) is formed by the United States, Canada, and Mexico.
1993	The European Union is formed, increasing economic ties among European nations.
1995	The World Trade Organization (WTO) is formed.
1997	The Asian financial crisis devastates Asian markets.
1999	About 50,000 activists in Seattle, Washington, protest against WTO policies and globalization.
2001	The WTO affirms the rights of governments to violate trade rules to protect the health of their citizens. A country can keep a product from entering if it is believed that the product can be harmful.
2005	World activists urge a "Global Call Against Poverty" to make trade fairer, cancel debts in less developed countries, and address the roots of poverty.
2007–2010	The financial crisis spreads across the world, resulting in a global recession.

Glossary

absolute advantage ability to make something more efficiently than the competition

bankrupt when people or companies cannot legally pay back the money they owe

boycott organized refusal to buy something, usually as a protest against the way the product was produced or farmed, or as a protest against the company itself

capital resources made by people; also, a money investment

capitalism economic system in which private individuals and corporations—rather than governments—produce and control the means of production

communist relating to a system in which the government plans and controls the economy

comparative advantage ability to produce something at a lower opportunity cost than the competition. Comparative advantage informs a country's or business's decision about what it should focus on producing for trade.

consultant expert who gives advice

consumer buyer

corporation large business organization

currency money

deforestation removal of trees in a forest or rain forest

demand how many goods people are willing to buy at the going price

developed refers to a country or part of the world with a strong economy and high standard of living

developing refers to a country or part of the world with an economy that is not as advanced as some developed parts of the world and in which many people do not have a high standard of living

economic theory ideas that explain how economies work

economics study of how society uses limited resources

economist person who studies how economies work

equilibrium price price at which the quantity demanded of a good and the quantity supplied are equal

exploit take advantage of

export sell goods to another country

free trade trade without restrictions

freelancer person who works independently

global worldwide

globalization way new technology has connected people and businesses around the world into a single marketplace

good item that can be bought and sold

Gross Domestic Product (GDP) measure of the total value of products and services produced in a country in a year

homesource employ people who work from home

immigration movement of people into a new country

import buy goods from another country

incentive reward for making certain choices

industry specific area of business

infrastructure systems that include services such as roads and communications systems

interest rate cost of borrowing money, expressed as a percentage of the borrowed amount

labor union organization representing the needs of workers as a group

monopoly market structure in which one firm decides the price and makes a product that does not have close substitutes

multinational in business, a company that does business in many different countries

offshoring moving parts of a business to another country

opportunity cost value lost by not pursuing something that is very profitable and instead pursuing something else

outsource hire another company to do work rather than having one's own company do it

pension fund that a company invests in on behalf of workers, to be paid when the workers retire

per capita per person

pollution substances that damage the air and water

producer someone who makes a good or a service

profit total money made by a business after the costs of producing something are subtracted

quota limit on the number of a type of good that can be imported to a country

recession decline in economic activity

regulate control how something operates

regulation rule or law that controls how something operates

resource thing used to make and buy goods and services

revenue money made after goods are sold

service performed action

stock share in a corporation

subsidy money that a government gives to a producer of local goods

supply how many goods someone is willing to sell at the going price

tariff fee that importers must pay for every good they take into another country

tax fee charged by a government— for example, on income or property owned

trade barrier something, such as a fee or restriction, that prevents free trade

trade deficit when a country imports more goods than it exports

trade imbalance when one country will be able to sell a large number of goods to another country, but will not want to buy a lot of goods from that country

trade surplus when a country exports more than it imports

trading bloc small group of countries that work together to improve trade through treaties

Find Out More

Books to read

Downing, David. *Global Business: Who Benefits? (Behind the News)*. Chicago: Heinemann Library, 2007.

Driscoll, William J. *Globalization and the Poor: Exploitation or Equalizer? (Sourcebook on Contemporary Controversies)*. New York: International Debate Education Association, 2003.

Gilman, Laura Anne. *Economics (How Economics Works)*. Minneapolis: Lerner, 2006.

Harris, Nathaniel. *Globalization (Ethical Debates)*. New York: Rosen, 2007.

Haugen, David M. *America's Global Influence (Opposing Viewpoints)*. Detroit: Greenhaven, 2007.

Haugen, David M. *Globalization (Opposing Viewpoints)*. Detroit: Greenhaven, 2010.

Websites

"Globalization 101"
www.globalization101.org
Learn more about all sides of the debate about globalization at this website, made just for students.

"The Globalization Website"
www.sociology.emory.edu/globalization/
This website provides different perspectives on globalization, as well as links to organizations and news related to globalization.

"Where We Stand: Globalization"
www.pbs.org/wnet/wherewestand/category/topics/globalization/
View videos about how globalization affects young people at this Public Broadcasting Service (PBS) website.

Index